CELTIC
A PRAYER
ILLUSTRATIONS
JOURNAL

The Northumbria Community

HarperCollins*Publishers*

Also available from the Northumbria Community

Celtic Daily Prayer
Celtic Night Prayer

HarperCollins*Publishers*
77–85 Fulham Palace Road, London w6 8jb

First published in 1997 by
HarperCollins*Publishers*

Copyright © 1997 The Northumbria Community

1 3 5 7 9 10 8 6 4 2

A catalogue record for this book is
available from the British Library

0 551 031026

Printed and bound in Great Britain by
Caledonian International Book Manufacturing Ltd, Glasgow

CONTENTS

ACKNOWLEDGEMENTS

With thanks to Nigel Evans for his pictures of the saints on pages 3, 43, 76, 112 and 142; Mary Fleeson for her drawings on pages 7, 31, 51, 93, 123, 145 and 155; Mark Fleeson for the chapter illustrations on pages 1, 41, 73, 109 and 137; Nancy Hammond for her calligraphy on pages 11, 101, 127, 131 and 163, and Beryl Wells for the borders on pages 5, 19, 27, 33, 45, 47, 59, 67, 79, 81, 103, 115, 117, 133, 143 and 157.

INTRODUCTION

In some of the early monasteries each monk used to dig one shovelful of earth from his own grave every day as a reminder of his own mortality. The same idea is found in the prayer in Psalm 90 which says: 'Teach us so to number our days that we may apply our hearts to wisdom!'

A prayer journal is the opportunity for me to take seriously what goes on in my heart. My impressions, struggles, longings, prayers – anything that seems important to me is committed to its pages.

Suppose a doctor or specialist were to say, 'You have only a month or so to live; how do you wish to use it?' Suddenly life assumes different priorities.

Each day of life is a day to be lived, and not missed out on. Each clear page is an opportunity as it waits to be filled.

Use this book as you choose, but it is not intended as a shopping list of items to buy, jobs to do or prayers for all the world. Any scrap of paper will do to off-load these. In this day and age paper is so cheap and plentiful we are in danger of under-valuing the privilege that is ours in using it. In times past whatever was of value had to be committed to memory. Most people never learned to read or write, and books were few and expensive, lovingly and painstakingly copied by hand.

...I study the Scriptures, puzzling over their meaning. I write books for the guidance of others. I eat little, and sleep little. When I eat I continue praying, and when I sleep my snores are songs of praise...

Picture a scholar-monk in his scriptorium or a hermit in his small cell in the woods, carefully copying sections of the Scriptures on to pieces of vellum.

I have a hut in the wood: no one knows of it except God ...
All around me the most beautiful music plays: the songs of
the birds, the lowing of cattle, the leaves rustling in the wind,
the cascade of the river. No king could hire such music with
gold: it is the music of Christ Himself, given freely.

On a blank page before him he decides to describe life as he sees it, or to pour out 'a prayer to the God of my life':

My soul's desire is to be freed from all fear and sadness, and
to share Christ's risen life. My soul's desire is to imitate my
King, and to sing His praises always. Dear Lord, you alone
know what my soul truly desires, and you alone can satisfy
those desires.

Pages like these survive.

God help my thoughts! They stray from me, setting off on the
wildest journeys. When I am in church, they run off like
naughty children, quarrelling, making trouble. My thoughts
can cross an ocean with a single leap: they can fly from earth
to heaven, and back again, in a single second. Dear Christ,
take hold of my thoughts. Bring my thoughts back to me, and
clasp me to yourself.

There was once a couple who noticed that a prophet often passed by the house where they lived. After some discussion they decided to set one room aside for him, furnish it simply, and then ask him to use it whenever he wished. Preparing this book feels to me very like the kind of work that couple carried out, so that Elisha the prophet would find somewhere ready for his use, a place comfortably set out, where he could lay down his baggage, kick off his sandals and feel at home. Unless after reading this you pick up a pen and make this book your own, it will just be wasted space.

Morton Kelsey describes this in his wonderful book, *Adventure Inward*:

> *My journal is a place where I can consider important questions and concerns. It is a place where I can pour forth my true feelings to God. I have discovered that, above all, God asks me to be myself and accepts me for so being. I have found my journal to be a holy place where I can meet God. During difficult times, I have received comfort just holding my journal in my hands, for it has come to represent to me my ongoing deepening pact with God.*

Kelsey continues to testify to the value of journalling as a reflective discipline:

> *My journal is a friend. Through it I have made discoveries which have enriched me and have enriched my relationships with others ...*
>
> *I do not have to be a specially gifted religious person to start keeping a record of my inner life. However, as I continue to use a journal I can learn how special and valuable I am to the divine Other who has made us all and who wants to draw us to the unsearchable riches of the kingdom. The possibilities described in former times are still open to those who will take the time and discipline to open themselves to the guiding Spirit of God and write down what they discover.*

I live on the Holy Island of Lindisfarne in north-Northumberland. It is known as a key site sacred to Celtic Christianity, but many of the saints of this area – such as Oswald, Hild and Cuthbert – were not Celts at all. And yet the faith they embraced was mediated to them by Irish monks from the island of Iona (off the coast of north-west Scotland). Their Christianity was characterized by simplicity of life, joy in all of creation, the expectation of 'miracles' as everyday events, generosity of spirit, honour in relationships, love of wisdom and its traditions and a contagious yielding to the God who had died for all people. Most were not called to die for what they believed, and so lived surrendered lives daily instead. I find my life daily informed in its reflection by these examples, these Celtic illustrations. I hope their light will be helpful also for you.

Andy Raine   *Holy Island*
The Northumbria Community   *1997*

What will
I do with
today?

wonder...

work...

awareness...

Today is mine. What will I do with it?
Throw it away. That's what I do with it,
Nine times out of ten.
The sun will shine. Am I a friend of it?
I wouldn't say I was a friend of it
Nine times out of ten.
What will I do with today?

A child reaches out to explore – so hungry for life, so full of wonder, and able to enjoy shape and colour and texture. The world is new, and wonder is a way of life. Where does the wonder go? How many layers of hurry and worry and trouble and seriousness do I need to shed to reach out again and embrace the wonder of today? Isaiah the prophet talks about people who see but don't really see, or hear but don't really hear. Today I want to be like a child again to see and *really* see with eyes that are wide and not strangers to tears.

The Celtic tradition of prayer is one of wonder and gratitude. It is also rooted firmly in everyday life. In the oral tradition, prayers have survived that are to be said while dressing, or while laying the fire, rowing a boat, milking a cow or going on a journey. The Mighty One, the God of Trinity, is not trapped in churches of wood or stone. He is ahead on the path, and blessing the boat, the byre, the crop. He is our close companion at every breaking of bread. He is with us in our work and in our weariness. The men and women of earlier generations would shake their heads when we complain of tiredness. They knew what hard work was.

Time has changed many things. Yet the words of Jesus telling us not to be anxious about anything are just as relevant to us today. Have we grown too sophisticated to need to put on Christ? His presence can be above us, beneath us, inside, outside, on left and right. We can put on Christ daily as we put on our clothes. It is all a matter of awareness. It means I am not alone, and that I recognize that however it may have been hurt, this is still my Father's world.

Oswald of Northumbria, like many kings, did not live to enjoy a peaceful old age. And yet the days of his reign brought great peace to the kingdom. As a lad, he was sent with his brothers to the monks of Iona, to find safety and gain an education. But Oswald had a far richer gain than his family had anticipated. He became a Christian and a man of prayer. His radical witness to his faith can be seen in the wooden cross he set up to kneel before at the battle of Heavenfield, in his urgent request for missionaries from Iona to come to preach to his people, and also in his willing service as an interpreter when Aidan began to declare the gospel without command of their language.

Oswald lived as a king, was married, fought as a warrior and enjoyed privilege, but took his responsibilities seriously. The finest picture we have of him is that when he was considering affairs of state or judging between petitioners his hands would instinctively turn palms upward to heaven, so used was he to praying at every opportunity. With open palms he offered each day, each moment, to the God of his life.

God be with me
in this Your day

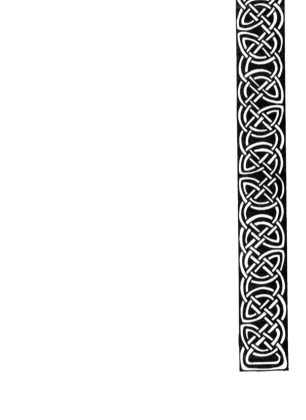

and the love and affection
of heaven be toward me.

THE EYE OF GOD
POURING UPON
ME RICHLY
GENEROUSLY

Help me to find my happiness
in friendly eyes,
in work well done!
in quietness born of trust,
and in the awareness
of Your presence in my spirit.

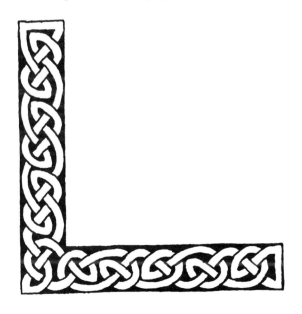

Do few things,
but do them well:

simple joys are holy.

His thoughts said,
'My work is not
important. Would it
matter very much if
a floor were left
unswept or a room
left untidied? Or if I
forgot to put flowers
for a guest, or
omitted some
tiny unimportant
courtesy?'

His Father said,
'Would if have
mattered very much if
a few people had been
left without wine at a
feast? But your Lord
turned water into
wine for them.' And
the son remembered
the words, Jesus took
a towel.

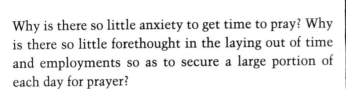

Why is there so little anxiety to get time to pray? Why is there so little forethought in the laying out of time and employments so as to secure a large portion of each day for prayer?

Why is there so much speaking, yet so little prayer? Why is there so much running to and fro, yet so little prayer? Why so much bustle and business, yet so little prayer? Why so many meetings with our fellow men, yet so few meetings with God?

Why so little being alone, so little
thirsting of the soul for the calm,
sweet hours of unbroken solitude,
when God and His child hold
fellowship together as if they
could never part?

It is the want of these solitary
hours that injures our own
growth in grace and that
renders our lives useless.

As the tide draws the waters
close in upon the shore,
make me an island, set apart,
alone with You, God,
holy to You.

Then with the turning of the tide
prepare me to carry Your presence
to the busy world beyond,
the world that rushes in on me
till the waters come again
and fold me back to You.

Lord, You have always given
strength for the coming day.
And though I am weak,
today I believe.

The troubles that weary me

I place into Your hands.

All that I do, Lord,
I place into Your hands.

There is a story told about a Jewish farmer who, through carelessness, did not get home before sunset one Sabbath and was forced to spend the day in the field waiting for sunset the next day before being able to return home. Upon his return home he was met by a rather perturbed rabbi who chided him for his carelessness. Finally the rabbi asked him: 'What did you do out there all day in the field? Did you at least pray?' The farmer answered: 'Rabbi, I am not a clever man. I don't know how to pray properly. What I did was simply to recite the alphabet all day and let God form the words for Himself.' When we come to pray we bring the alphabet of our lives. If our hearts and minds are full of warmth, love, enthusiasm, song and dance, then these are the letters we bring. If they are full of tiredness, despair, blandness, pain and boredom, then those are our letters. Bring them. Spend them. Celebrate them. It is God's task to make the words!

Show me what blessing it is that I have work to do.

And sometimes, and most of all
when the day is overcast and my courage faints,
let me hear Your voice, saying,
'you are my beloved one in whom I am well pleased.'

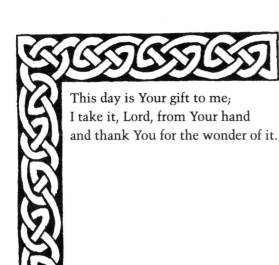

This day is Your gift to me;
I take it, Lord, from Your hand
and thank You for the wonder of it.

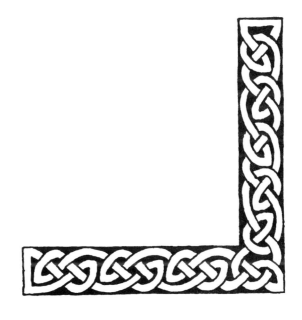

One of the best known of the Desert Fathers of fourth-century Egypt, St Sarapion the Sindonite, travelled once on a pilgrimage to Rome. Here he was told of a celebrated recluse, a woman who lived always in one room, never going out. Sceptical about her way of life – for he was a great wanderer – Sarapion called on her and asked:

'Why are you sitting here?'

To this she replied:

'I am not sitting. I am on a journey.'

If you want to live life free,
take your time, go slowly.

What am I here for?

hopes...
visions...
promises...

If I am always driven by what is urgent, it will be easy to be always busy and on the move, but with no real sense of direction. If I have no goals, how would I even recognize them were I to reach them? What are my hopes, and how might they be realized? What is my heart really set on? (Often my life is spent in responding only to what is immediate, instead of the things I claim are of importance to me.) What *am* I here for?

It is usually helpful for me to try to list the things I hope for – especially if I can be very honest. It is a list I will return to, perhaps many times. Some of these hopes will be realized with time, work and prayer. In fact, God is the best and most willing custodian of my hopes. Some of my desires are met and fulfilled, but very differently from how I imagined. Some hopes eventually turn to disappointments anyway, but it will be crucial to invite His interest, involvement and intervention at every stage.

Some visions die for a time, but emerge again in a different form. These things are often very dear to our hearts, and it seems the whole of us is invested in seeing them take shape. 'Can I not work on you as a potter would?' says the Lord. 'Yes,' I say. Sometimes I say it joyfully, sometimes painfully, but I quickly learn that it is wiser to trust Him completely.

Keeping promises is very important. Promises we make to others or those they make to us can be like posts – stakes sunk very deeply in the ground of our life. Sometimes a promise has to take the whole weight of a person, so it must be planted deep and firm. What promises do you depend on? Who in your life depends on you keeping the promises you have made? Is there anything you have promised to God?

When I was still young I heard a little song from South Africa which said,

> When the Lord calls, I will answer:
> I'll be somewhere working for my Lord.

It became a fixed post in my life that if I made that promise, God would help me to keep it.

In the words of Jeremiah we read: 'Set up the way marks, so you may return the same way' and 'Ask for the old paths where the good way is, and walk there. That is where you will find rest for your soul.'

Boisil's days passed quietly in the hidden ways of a monastic. To live his life close to God, and in harmony with heaven, was what mattered. He had chosen especially to steep himself in the gospel written by John, the closest disciple of all to Jesus, and the one towards whom the Celtic branch of the Church had a special affection and loyalty. By now he readily sensed God's purposes and priorities, and so when he first saw Cuthbert approaching the door of the monastery at Melrose he recognized that here was no ordinary vocation and that God had specially chosen this young man to be His servant. So Boisil made it his priority to love and encourage him. Faithfully, urgently, he imparted all he could: the fruit of his life of prayer, study, and loving service of others. Boisil trained him well, and soon Cuthbert was chosen to work in Ripon, where he stayed for some time.

When the plague came, both men were struck down by it. Boisil was adamant that Cuthbert would recover, but saw that now his own days were numbered, and this he accepted peacefully. The two men chose to spend the last week of Boisil's life reading John's gospel together, and sharing their insights.

Boisil died as he lived, leaning closely on Jesus. Before his death, he reminded Cuthbert – in whom he had invested so much – that God had important work for him to do, which would one day bring him the responsibilities of a bishop in His church. This was a significant word in Cuthbert's life, because without it he would have refused to leave his hermitage on the Inner Farne to care for the needs of the people in the surrounding countryside. Cuthbert had taken Boisil's words of counsel and knowledge and hidden them in his heart. It is important to have vision. To choose between good and evil takes wisdom and character; but to choose between two goods requires vision and discernment.

'Follow Me!'

'… If I did follow You,
where would I be going?'

'With Me!'

Lord, You have always marked
the road for the coming day.
And though it may be hidden
today I believe.

I place into Your hands, Lord,
the choices that I face.

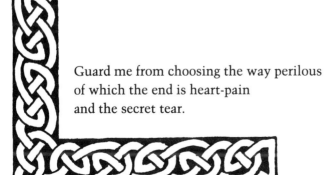

Guard me from choosing the way perilous
of which the end is heart-pain
and the secret tear.

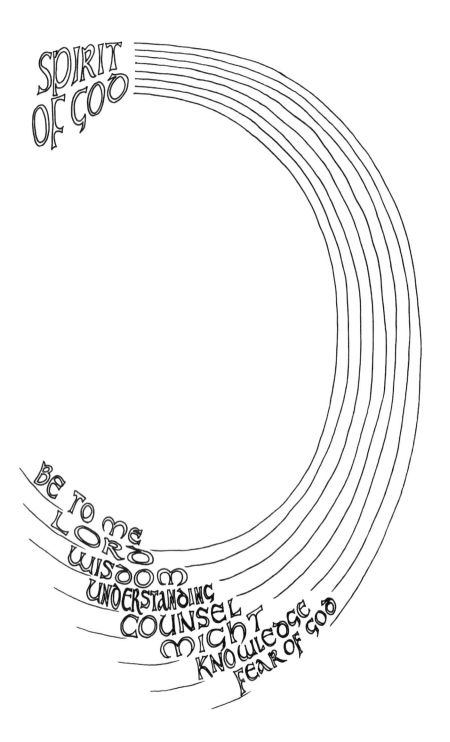

SPIRIT OF GOD

BE TO ME LORD
WISDOM
UNDERSTANDING
COUNSEL
MIGHT
KNOWLEDGE
FEAR OF GOD

Will You be my guidance
in my words and actions?

Stay with me forever
and keep me on the right path.

The Holy Spirit
entrusts things
in every age to
particular people.
Some things are so
firmly rooted in my
heart that if I didn't
practise them, I
couldn't even claim
to be me anymore.

All that I am, Lord,

I place into Your hands.

If you want your dream to be,
build it slow and surely.

Lord, You have always given
bread for the coming day.
And though I am poor,
today I believe.

Everything I work for

I place into Your hands.

Small beginnings,
greater ends.
Heartfelt work grows purely.

Everything I hope for

I place into Your hands.

May I feel Your presence
at the heart of my desire,
and so know it for Your desire for me.
Thus shall I prosper,
thus see that my purpose is from You,
thus have power to do the good which endures.

Day by day,
stone by stone,
build your secret slowly.

Day by day,
you'll grow too;
you'll know heaven's glory!

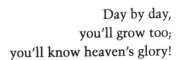

my
soul
waits

disappointments

silence

trust

After the long months of pregnancy, and then a difficult journey through snow and blizzards, we were finally in the labour room where my wife was to give birth to our first child. I put her chosen long-playing album in the tape recorder, and wondered which song would be playing for the birth. All I could do was wait, and be fully present to her. But every time the tape finished I would press REWIND and think, 'Surely this time must be the last time.'

Waiting times are like that. They go on for ever, especially if we are uncertain of what is at the end of that waiting. Is everyone all right? Have I got the job? Did I pass? Are there any messages for me? When are things going to change? All we can do is wait, be fully present and available.

People say, 'If I'd known things would turn out so well I would never have worried.' Others say, 'If I'd known all this trouble was waiting round the corner I'd never have slept at night just thinking about it.'

But we don't know what lies ahead; the future is not predetermined. Even to God it exists only as possibilities. He truly allows us to choose. We can co-operate with what He plans or take residence in the 'instead-zone'.

Life is not a series of calmly presented happinesses. It is a mixture of joy and catastrophe, pain and confusion, fulfilment and frustration. One life may be different from another, but none is exempt from difficulty. That is why Jesus lived as a real human being, year after year and moment by moment. In doing so He took no short cuts, but shared in our struggle.

God the Father says to us:

Once did my Son live your life, and by His faithfulness did show my mind, my kindness, and my truth to all. But now He is come to my side and you must take His place.

A child in pain does not understand. Accusing eyes beg the grown-up to take the hurt away. Sometimes all the loving father or mother can do is hold the little one very tightly and wait for the hurting to go away.

God does care. He is there, immediate and loving, but very often silent.

Words of promise give us perspective; there *will* be an end to this time of waiting. One beautiful example of this is the story of Iona. Columba saw by the Spirit of God that the work he had started there with his island monastery would one day be overturned, but even then it would not be lost for ever. He wrote:

> *Iona of my heart,*
> *Iona of my love,*
> *instead of monks' voices*
> *shall be lowing of cattle,*
> *but ere the world comes to an end*
> *Iona shall be as it was.*

With the foundation of the Iona Community, the re-building of the ruined monastery, and with the strong and growing influence of the Celtic tradition of Christianity which Columba so exemplifies, this prophecy is already being fulfilled.

But for how many years did the ruins lie silent? How unlikely it once seemed that anything significant would arise from Iona again, or that it would see a committed, serving community, giving witness and hospitality, and marking hours of prayer!

The Hebridean song of Christmas speaks of the labour before birth – even the birth of the Christ-child – and says:

> *This night is the long night ...*

Celtic Christianity was known for its double monasteries, where men and women celibates lived peacefully side by side, always under the authority of a woman. In the case of the famous monastery at Whitby, that woman was the Abbess Hild, and her foundation was chosen to host the council called by Oswy, the

King. His royal household at Bamburgh had been divided in its practice, with the Queen and her attendants following a Roman calendar. The discrepancies arising, especially when it came to feasting and solemn fasting, were a domestic nightmare – a recurring and drastic inconvenience.

Abbess Hild was well acquainted with the speakers representing both sides of the dispute the council addressed. As a young princess, she had herself been baptized by the Roman missionary Paulinus; but it was the gentle Aidan from Iona who had come to Lindisfarne and urged her to live her vocation here in her homeland of Northumbria. Aidan had soon found the measure of her people, and his quiet, sure faith impressed all he met. This was still her example and inspiration. The love for God that burned in him so brightly had been ignited in countless others across the kingdom, even during his lifetime, and it fell to Hild and others in whom he had invested so much to build strongly on the foundations he had left them. The council which began today should only serve to encourage them further in this process.

Colman was the present leader of the community on the island of Lindisfarne, a good man who lived and spoke simply, warmly defending the way of life taught by Aidan and Columba of Iona and all who had gone before them.

The surprise speaker who eloquently opposed him was a young monk named Wilfrid, himself educated under Aidan, but recently returned from a long visit to Rome. Colman listened aghast as Wilfrid ridiculed Celtic Christianity as outmoded and rebellious. He advocated immediate conformity to Roman practices. Wilfrid took care to mention the Roman church's loyalty to Peter who surely approved of anyone who helped the cause of his successors. And did not Peter stand at the doorway of heaven as each soul approached? A look of terror passed across King Oswy's face.

Hild listened in disbelief, for suddenly, abruptly, the verdict had been spoken. The king had decided in favour of the Roman party. From now on the distinctive Celtic practices and traditions which she had grown to love and respect would be outlawed. Abbot Colman said that he and many of the Lindisfarne monks would leave and return to Iona, or go off in search of a kingdom where they could live their faith and witness in the ways they had been taught. It all seemed so unnecessary, too, this insistence on conformity. Here, there had always been a tolerance towards visitors who practised their Christianity differently, so if the King had decided to uphold the Celtic practices, things would largely have continued as before. But such courtesy would not be shown in return. Now the monastic tonsures must be adjusted, the date for the celebration of Easter altered to coincide with the fashionable practice in Rome. The bishops would now have authority based on land and territory, instead of relationship, and would have powers to rival any abbot.

It felt like walls of stone appearing where once there had only been hills, forests and rolling seas. Hild's heart was heavy, and the sense of foreboding could not be shaken. And yet, God had allowed it; and He surely had not deserted them or left them to shrivel up and despair. So what if structures had to change, her heart would still be fixed on Him. This freedom of spirit, this instinct to respond creatively – even to unwelcome challenge – nobody could take this away from them; it belonged to all those who chose to stay and work, ensuring that all was not lost. Today was a dark day, and it might well grow darker yet, but joy must come again. Joy cannot be suppressed – it is the gift of God.

Pray as you can,
not as you can't!

There is a contemplative in all of us,
almost strangled but still alive,
who craves quiet enjoyment of the Now,
and longs to touch the seamless garment of silence
which makes whole.

We need to protect each
other's times for silence.
Give us the courage to say
'Leave me alone with God'
as much as may be.

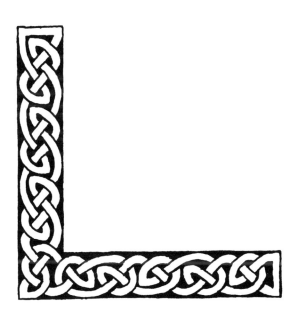

If we practised silence
a little bit more,
then when we did speak
we'd have something to say.

I will wait for the Lord.
My soul waits,
And in His word
Do I hope.

Lord, You have always kept
me safe in trials,
And now, tried as I am,
Today I believe.

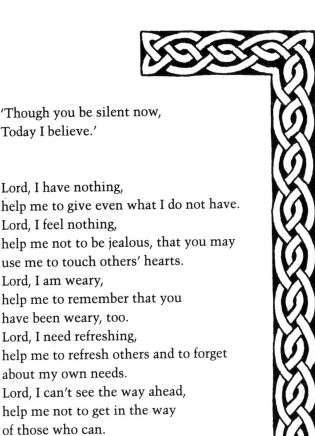

'Though you be silent now,
Today I believe.'

Lord, I have nothing,
help me to give even what I do not have.
Lord, I feel nothing,
help me not to be jealous, that you may
use me to touch others' hearts.
Lord, I am weary,
help me to remember that you
have been weary, too.
Lord, I need refreshing,
help me to refresh others and to forget
about my own needs.
Lord, I can't see the way ahead,
help me not to get in the way
of those who can.
Lord, I am disappointed,
help me not to bring disappointed
to others.
Lord, I have no one to help me,
help me to trust in you,
Lord, I can't see you, yet you see me,
help me to remember that.
Lord, I am not worthy to receive you,
but only say the word and I shall be healed.

You have a little strength,
and have kept My word
and not denied
My name.

Keep me close to You, Lord,

Keep me close to You.

Lord, You have always given
peace for the coming day.
And though of anxious heart,
today I believe.

As my Father, take care of me,
and listen to my prayers
and give me a place
to live inside Your heart.

Into Your hands I commend my spirit;
I give it to You with all the love of my heart,

for I love You, Lord,
and so need to give myself,
to surrender myself into Your hands
with a trust beyond all measure,
because You are my Father.

I believe I shall see the goodness of the Lord
in the land of the living.

By day the Lord directs His love,

at night His song is with me –
a prayer to the God of my life.

monsters and mysteries

dreams

in the

night

'There are, it may be, so many kinds of voices ... and none of them is without signification,' says Paul the apostle in his famous letter to the Christian community at Corinth. If we apply this observation to the language of our dreams it is obviously a true statement.

I can immediately think of several sorts of dream recollected upon waking. There is the 'joining up all the loose ends' sort of dream in which unfinished conversation, unaddressed tasks, whatever was mentioned, whoever was noticed but not given attention to, suddenly becomes the focus of our attention. Maybe this is the brain tidying things up so the waking mind has a clear desk to begin the next day. Even this can be interesting. Tom Stoppard's play *Rozencrantz and Guildenstern Are Dead* uses this idea, and by putting two incidental characters centre-stage gives a completely different perspective on Shakespeare's *Hamlet*. A fresh perspective is a valuable gift in its own right.

A recurring dream will always be worth remembering and recording. It draws our attention to something which needs addressing by being resolved or finally understood. To talk about it or write it down is profoundly useful, as the words we use to describe these impressions very often show we have understood more than we have realized. If not, then the language or images of the dream can wait to be unlocked later on. When the meaning is found it will be clear, not contrived or confusing.

A nightmare is also worth examining in daylight. What was it that was so terrifying or unpleasant? Was it the sense of powerlessness or paralysis? Was it being unable to shout out? We call this process of examination 'naming the monster'. Once the monster is identified, its power and capabilities can be examined and assessed. Then, when that particular monster jumps out from the shadows, instead of being terrorized we can say, 'Oh, it's you again!'

It is said that the preacher Smith Wigglesworth woke one night to find his bed rattling. A menacing figure was at the foot of the bed, shaking it. 'Oh, it's only you, Satan,' said Smith Wigglesworth and turned over to go back to sleep.

All fear is based upon a lie of some sort. If we deal with the lie, then the fear must die. Fear is a big bully, but the one true God reveals Himself as perfect love, the love that overthrows fear. With fear out of the way our problems may not disappear, but they can now be seen for what they are and not as what they are not. The dream has done us a kindness if it identifies subconscious fears that have affected our waking existence.

All dreams mean something, but in many cases the meaning is nothing very significant. Those who find they can regularly recall at least part of what they dream will probably flick through them as they would a magazine, on the look-out for anything which particularly catches their interest. Their waking life will hopefully provide more to engage their attention.

From time to time a person will have a dream that is very different indeed. It is vivid and compelling and there is no choice but to take it seriously. Like a good story book, film or music video, we give it our full attention. What we make of it is a further question. This dream must be recorded and remembered. Sometimes it will be a 'numinous' dream with a message or impression that clearly comes from beyond our own being or consciousness. In sleep I may be more receptive to spiritual impressions than my defensive waking mind allows me to be. It is good to ask God to guard our minds for us while we sleep, and then enjoy the freedom to fly or sing or do battle, to travel or meet up with long-forgotten acquaintances. Often the person we unexpectedly dream about, or the person we suddenly feel called to pray for, has been thinking about us, or will make contact with us within a day or two.

As in C. S. Lewis's Narnia stories, where there is a land to be reached through the back of a wardrobe, in dreams we may meet with all kinds of persons and experiences, good and bad. Sometimes we find only wood at the back of the wardrobe, but at other times it is the edge of a forest in a world where an ordinary child is given wisdom and royal responsibility.

Caedmon loved to listen. Music thrilled him, and other people's stories, songs and ballads carried him along as helplessly as a small boat on a rising tide. But he couldn't play a note on the harp. Nor could he sing a note in tune. If he tried to join in with a song when he was a child everyone else was unable to keep singing. Besides, he could never remember any words. He couldn't even tell a joke and get it right. His head got all confused, and the words tumbled out back to front.

So a night like tonight was torture for him. Heaven and hell, that's what it was. To hear each person share a song, to listen to the music of the harp as it was passed along, strummed by one, touched gently by another – nothing could be sweeter. But the nearer it came to Caedmon's turn the more a sickness rose from his stomach, and his bowels stirred uneasily. At the last possible moment he could he would run out of the hall.

Once outside he went straight to the cattle shed to check on his beasts, then threw himself down on his bed, and passed into a fitful sleep.

In his dream a man stood before him. 'Sing for me, Caedmon,' he said. 'Sing for me.'

'I can't sing,' Caedmon protested. 'Why do you think I'm out here in the cattle shed, instead of at the feast?'

'Sing anyway, sing for me.'

'I don't know what to sing.'

'Sing about the beginning of the world, and sing about creation.'

So Caedmon sang a song of praise to the Guardian of heaven, the Father of glory. And in his dream he was able to sing ... a song so beautiful it could make you cry.

When he awoke, the song was still with him, and he sang it for God and for himself. He sang it for the steward of all the farmlands of the abbey. He sang it for Abbess Hild herself when the steward told her what had happened. He sang it for all the scholars and holy men and women of the abbey the Lady Hild had called for. He sang it for the people of Whitby and everyone in the countryside round about.

Now someone else looked after the cattle while whoever could read spoke aloud the Scriptures and translated them for Caedmon. Each night he sang aloud the things he had heard until a new song was prepared, explaining the Bible to his people in their own language. And now for all his life his mouth spoke out the truths that filled his heart.

I will praise the Lord who counsels me.

Even at night my heart instructs me.

Christian morality clearly
requires each of us to deal
with our own inner chaos
so that it will not slip out
of its space-time container
and affect others.

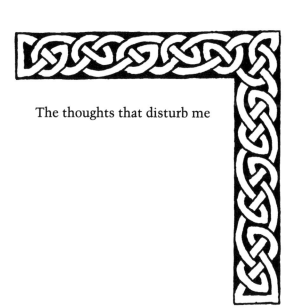

The thoughts that disturb me

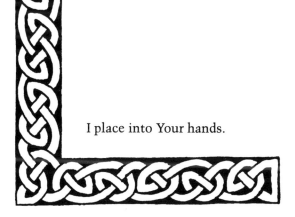

I place into Your hands.

O Christ, son of the living God,
may Your holy angels guard our sleep,
may they watch us as we rest.
Let them reveal to us in our dreams
visions of Your glorious truth.

Master Speak!

Your servant is listening

I have heard you calling in the night

Be my eyes, O king of creation.
Fill my life with understanding and patience.

Will You be my mind every night and every day?
Sleeping or awake,
fill me with Your love.

In the shadow of your wings
I will sing your praises
O LORD

How precious to me
are Your thoughts, O God!
How vast is the sum of them!

Were I to count them,
they would outnumber the grains of sand.
When I awake,
I am still with You.

Beyond these shores ...
into the darkness ...

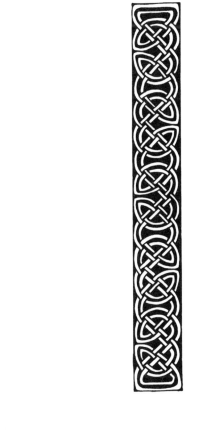

this boat may sail.

I do not think that I shall fear Thee

when I see Thee face to face.

doorkeeping -hospitality of the heart

prayer
for
other
people

For many, it can be hard to begin writing in a journal or opening their heart to God, because as soon as they become still, concerns about other people rush into their minds and clamour for their attention. God does not fail to notice what is on our heart, and there will be times when it is appropriate to hold these concerns before God, to bring the people we care for to Him. In Israel, twelve engraved stones were set into the breastplate of the High Priest so the names of each of the tribes of the people he served would be worn on his heart, and carried before God.

As we pray, we try to be open to hearing what is on God's heart as well. It is Him we prepare to encounter, asking His presence to surround us. Using the ancient Celtic 'caim' or circling prayer we may say,

> Circle me, God.
> Keep my attention on You; keep distractions out.
> Circle me, God.
> Keep quietness in; keep anxiety out.

The same simple prayer-exercise can focus us in our prayer for others – especially when we don't know what to pray on their behalf. (For example, 'Circle my friend who is in trouble, God. Keep wisdom in; keep other people's noses out!') Use a page of circles, and you will soon become accustomed to the idea of praying in this way.

The world in which we pray, and live, and journal, is full of people. Some of us can disregard this more readily than others. Morton Kelsey writes:

> Whenever one's record of the inner life takes the place of human relationships, one is in danger. Our journal writing should make us more outgoing, loving and relatable, or else something has gone wrong. A journal is no substitute for living.
>
> Some people are so close to the inner world that they should be encouraged away from journal keeping and out

into relationships with people and things. One person's meat can be another's poison. Journal keeping can be dangerous when it becomes an escape from living rather than a place of reflection which leads to more adequate living.

The Celtic monastery was a place to be reflective, and seek to know God more and more. In fact, many monasteries and hermitages were in wild, remote and inaccessible places where the monastic or solitary could give their whole self to prayer and spiritual battle with few interruptions. Visitors were to be greeted, honoured and cared for as if they were Christ Himself. This was easier to remember if visitors were few, or if they were pleasant company.

It is said that in Ireland one Brother called Cronan became distressed when he realized that a visitor looking for him in Sean Ross had been unable to find him. He moved his whole establishment to Roscrea in consequence.

'I shall not remain in a desert place,' he said, 'where strangers and poor folk are unable to find me readily. But here by the public highway I shall live, where they are able to reach me easily.'

Soon many Christian settlements were founded along the main roads of Ireland with a conscious desire to be able to offer hospitality to wayfarers, and serve those in need.

It is important not just to welcome people into your home, but to take folk into your heart, too. As a small boy, I remember my dad speaking of a favourite poem by Sam Walter Foss. It begins like this:

*Let me live in a house by the side of the road
where the race of men go by –
the men who are good and the men who are bad,
as good and bad as I.
I would not sit in a scorner's seat*

or hurl the cynic's ban;
let me live in a house by the side of the road
and be a friend to man.

My dad didn't just love that poem: he lived it.

Praying for other people is a hospitality of the heart. Just like monastic hospitality, it is a discipline. But it's also a reflex; so prayerful concern for others should characterize any whose interior life is developing. We may commit ourselves to be available, but have no way of estimating how profound the effects may be on another life. When Oswald and his brothers were taken in by the Iona monks, the fugitives were offered safety and schooling. Little did the monks realize that by continuing in their daily way of life under the close scrutiny of these foreign youngsters, greater evangelistic consequences would result than the work of any mission team they knew of. Whole kingdoms would be reached because of the light young Oswald could see shining through the monks he met on Iona. They were essentially door-keepers – opening the way into the presence of God.

Samuel Moor Shoemaker, in *I stand by the Door*, describes the problem of people disappearing so far into their own interiority, or going so deep even in their awareness of God that they forget to help

the people who have not yet even found the door,
or the people who want to run away again from God.

He says,

As for me, I shall take my old, accustomed place, near enough to God to hear Him, and know He is there, but not so far from others that I don't hear them and remember they are there, too.

A journal can be the place where we make connections from our everyday life, or our particular place of wrestling and struggle, and recognize that this is the gateway to heaven, a door from our own world into that other which is truly home.

W. Muir wrote this prayer and attributed it to Columba:

... to me allow
that I may keep a door in Paradise,
that I may keep even the smallest door,
the farthest door, the darkest, coldest door,
the door that is least used, the stiffest door,
if so it be but in Thy house, O God,
if so it be that I may see Thy glory,
even afar, and hear Thy voice, O God,
and know that I am with Thee,
Thee, O God.

Columba breathed deeply, nodded and continued to write:

And I would rather be a doorkeeper in the house of my God
than dwell in the tents of the wicked.

His eyes scanned the page of the book of psalms that he was transcribing. This one was a particular favourite. *Selah* – pause and ponder awhile. Live as a man whose strength is in You. The vows he made, and lived. Obedience had brought him far from the Ireland he loved to calm his war-like pride, and learn the ways of peace. Always he thought of home, and prayed for the people of Ireland. Of course, he had no sons by the flesh. The vow of celibacy he had taken freed him from that. 'My heart and flesh cry aloud to the living God.' A smile broke over his face as he remembered the distress of his friend Lugne. Poor Lugne's wife had decided to leave him, offer herself as a nun –

do anything other than share a bed with him any longer, so greatly had she come to loathe him! Columba had agreed to pray, took them gladly on his heart for one whole night. Some miracle occurred, for from that night she loved her husband tenderly and would not be parted from him. Friends – how he valued them. And in the community here on Iona he had many sons, heirs to a rich heritage in God. Riches – in poverty. Jacob was an exile too, with a stone for his pillow he saw heaven open. Heaven so close, and here his sons, his brothers, his friends. He prayed for them all, and blessed them, speaking aloud the words on the page he had transcribed:

They go from strength to strength – each one appears before God.

He picked up the pen, and again began writing.

O Son of Mary,
how wonderful Your friendliness to me!
How deep! How unchanging!
Help me to pass it on.

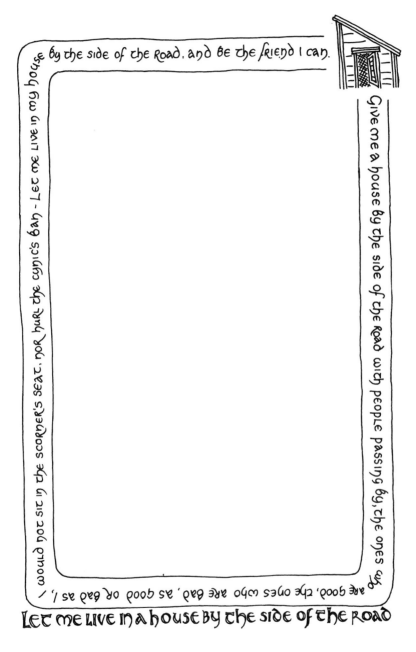

by the side of the road, and be the friend I can.

Give me a house by the side of the road with people passing by, the ones who

are good, the ones who are bad, as good or bad as I, / I would not sit in the scorner's seat, nor hurt the cynic's ban – Let me live in my house

LET ME LIVE IN A HOUSE BY THE SIDE OF THE ROAD

145

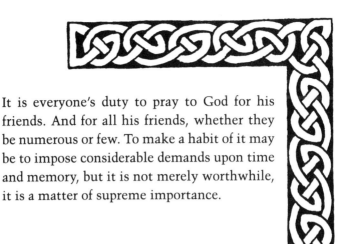

It is everyone's duty to pray to God for his friends. And for all his friends, whether they be numerous or few. To make a habit of it may be to impose considerable demands upon time and memory, but it is not merely worthwhile, it is a matter of supreme importance.

If you've only a handful of friends, it won't take long, and if you're one of the lucky ones, with more friends that you can remember all at once, card-index them. Pray for them in instalments, but pray for them.

Each that I pray for
I place into Your hands.

Each that I care for

I place into Your hands.

My dear ones, O God,
bless Thou and keep,
in every place where they are.

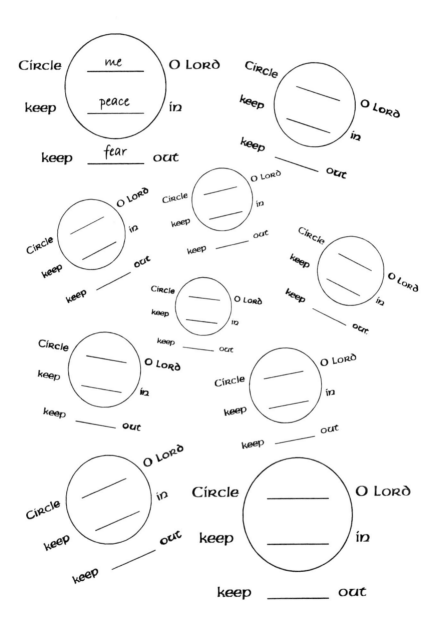

Circle ___me___ O Lord

keep ___peace___ in

keep ___fear___ out

Circle O Lord

keep in

keep out

Circle O Lord

keep in

keep out

Circle O Lord

keep in

keep out

Circle O Lord

keep in

keep out

Circle O Lord

keep in

keep out

Circle O Lord

keep in

keep out

Circle O Lord

keep in

keep out

Circle O Lord

keep in

keep out

Circle _____ O Lord

keep _____ in

keep _____ out

In relationships at their best,
people catch a glimpse of God.

The abbot Macarius said:

'If we dwell upon the
harms that have been
wrought on us by people,
we amputate from our
mind the power of
dwelling upon God.'

Setting our face towards relationship
is choosing to be broken and blessed.

See that ye be
at peace—⁖
amone yourselves,
my children, and
LOVE ONE ANOTHER
Follow the example—
of good men of old
**AND GOD WILL
COMFORT YOU
AND HELP YOU**
Both in this world
and in the world
which is to come—⁖ ⁖

LIST OF SOURCES

PAGE	SOURCE
VII, VIII	From *Celtic Fire*, Robert Van de Weyer, Darton, Longman & Todd, 1990.
IX	*Adventure Inward, Christian Growth through Personal Journal Writing*, Morton Kelsey, Augsburg, 1980.
2	'What will I do with today?', lyrics by Leslie Bricusse, from the film *Goodbye, Mr Chips*. © International Music Publishers Ltd.
5	Alistair Maclean, *Hebridean Altars*, Moray Press, 1937, p. 62.
7	From A. Carmichael, *Carmina Gadelica*, Scottish Academic Press.
9	Alistair Maclean, *Hebridean Altars*, p. 88.
11	Psalm 90.
13	Song performed by Donovan, from the film *Brother Sun, Sister Moon*. © The Famous Music Corporation.
15	Amy Carmichael, *His Thoughts Said, His Father Said*, SPCK, 1941.
17	Horatius Bonar, *Words to Winners of Souls*, American Tract Society, 1950.
19	Ibid.
21	Ibid.
23	Andy Raine, Aidan Liturgy, *Celtic Night Prayer*, Marshall Pickering, 1996, p. 34.
25	'Expressions of Faith', from *God's Love Casts Out Fear, A Week of Prayer for Christian Unity*, originally prepared in Italy and translated for the British Council of Churches Week of Prayer for Christian Unity, 1988.

27   Andy Raine, Oswald liturgy, *Celtic Night Prayer*, p. 29.

29   Ibid.

31   Ronald Rolheiser, *Forgotten Among the Lilies*, Spire, 1990, p. 161. Reproduced by permission of Hodder & Stoughton.

33   Alistair Maclean, *Hebridean Altars*, p. 45.

35   Ibid., p. 63.

37   Fr Kallistos Ware, *The Orthodox Way*, Mowbray, 1981, p. 37.

39   Song from *Brother Sun, Sister Moon*, performed by Donovan.

43   'Set up the way marks, so you may return the same way' (Jeremiah 31:21); 'Ask for the old paths where the good way is, and walk there. That is where you will find rest for your soul' (Jeremiah 6:16).

45   Anon.

47   'Expressions of Faith', see above.

49   Andy Raine, Oswald Liturgy, *Celtic Night Prayer*, p. 29.

51   Isaiah 11:2.

53   Gaelic adaptation of 'Be Thou My Vision' by Hugh Brennan; English translation by Adodh ó Dugáin, from *Journey Into the Morn*, Iona. Reproduced by permission of SGO Music Publishing Ltd.

55   Mike Shaughnessey.

57   Andy Raine, Oswald Liturgy, *Celtic Night Prayer*, p. 29.

59   Song from *Brother Sun, Sister Moon*, performed by Donovan.

61   'Expressions of Faith', see above.

63   Andy Raine, Oswald Liturgy, *Celtic Night Prayer*, p. 29.

65   Song from *Brother Sun, Sister Moon*, performed by Donovan.

67   Andy Raine, Oswald Liturgy, *Celtic Night Prayer*, p. 29.

69   Alistair Maclean, *Hebridean Altars*, p. 149.

71   Song from *Brother Sun, Sister Moon*, performed by Donovan.

74   Alistair Maclean, *Hebridean Altars*, p. 53.

75   'This night is...' – from the *Carmina Gadelica*.
79   Dom Chapman.
81   Alan P. Torey.
83   Andy Raine, Aidan Liturgy, *Celtic Night Prayer*, p. 33.
85   John T. Skinner.
87   Psalm 130:5.
89   'Expressions of Faith', see above.
91   'Though you...' – 'Expressions of Faith', see above;
      'Lord, I have nothing...' – Hugh Barney, from *Celtic
      Night Prayer*, p. 222.
93   Revelation 3:8.
95   Andy Raine, Oswald Liturgy, *Celtic Night Prayer*, p. 30.
97   'Expressions of Faith', see above.
99   Gaelic adaptation of 'Be Thou My Vision' by Hugh
      Brennan; English translation by Adodh ó Dugáin, from
      Journey Into the Morn, Iona.
101   Traditional Celtic prayer, perhaps most popularly known
      in this form by David Adam, from *The Edge of Glory*,
      SPCK, 1985.
103   Charles de Foucauld.
105   Psalm 27:13.
107   Psalm 42:8.
110   'There are, it may be, so many kinds of voices ... and
      none of them is without signification' (1 Corinthians
      14:10).
115   Psalm 16:7.
117   Morton Kelsey.
119   Andy Raine, Oswald Liturgy, *Celtic Night Prayer*, p. 29.
121   Andy Raine, Aidan Compline, *Celtic Night Prayer*,
      pp. 5–6.
123   1 Samuel 3:3–5, 9–10.
125   Gaelic adaptation of 'Be Thou My Vision' by Hugh
      Brennan; English translation by Adodh ó Dugáin, from
      Journey Into the Morn, Iona.
127   Psalm 63:7.
129   Psalm 139:17–18.